THE LANGUAGES OF PROGRAMMING

Author: Dr Dharini Balasubramaniam • Illustrator: Luke Séguin-Magee

WAYLAND

First published in Great Britain in 2025 by Wayland

Text © Dharini Balasubramaniam 2025
Illustrations © Hodder and Stoughton 2025
Design © Hodder and Stoughton 2025

The right of Dharini Balasubramaniam to be identified as the Author of this Work has been asserted by the Author in accordance with the Copyright Designs and Patents Act 1988

All rights reserved.

Commissioning Editor: Grace Glendinning
Editor: Amy Pimperton
Designer: Lisa Peacock
Illustrations: Luke Séguin-Magee

ISBN: 978 1 5263 2799 4 HBK
ISBN: 978 1 5263 2801 4 PBK
ISBN: 978 1 5263 2800 7 EBOOK

Printed and bound in China.

Wayland, an imprint of
Hachette Children's Group
Part of Hodder and Stoughton
Carmelite House
50 Victoria Embankment
London EC4Y 0DZ

An Hachette UK Company
www.hachette.co.uk
www.hachettechildrens.co.uk

The authorised representative in the EEA is
Hachette Ireland, 8 Castlecourt Centre,
Dublin 15, D15 XTP3, Ireland
(email: info@hbgi.ie)

Every effort has been made by the Publishers to ensure that the websites in this book are suitable for children, that they are of the highest educational value, and that they contain no inappropriate or offensive material. However, because of the nature of the Internet, it is impossible to guarantee that the contents of these sites will not be altered. We strongly advise that Internet access is supervised by a responsible adult.

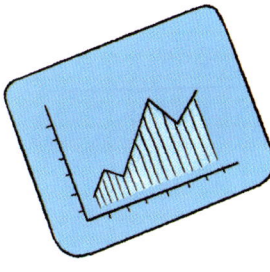

CONTENTS

What *is* a language?	4–5
Languages can come naturally ...	6–7
... or languages can be constructed	8–9
Language types for CS	10–11
Even more languages!	12–13
It's all syntax and semantics	14–15
Ways of programming	16–17
Choose your language	18–19
Programming is a process	20–21
Tools to make our work easier	22–23
Case study: Blocks vs Python	24–25
The future of programming languages	26-27
Pioneer portraits	28–30
Further information	30
Glossary	31
Quiz yourself!	32
Index	32

What *is* a language?

Humans share information, thoughts and questions all the time. Although we don't always think about it, we do this using languages.

Define: language

A **language** is a system of communication that we use to express ourselves. In other words, it's how we exchange information and ideas.

Daily life

Many of the things we do in our lives – including studying, working and making friends – are made possible by languages. These activities often require us to communicate with others or record (write down and keep) our ideas and views.

We can record or communicate our ideas in many ways.

Note-taking   Emailing   Chatting

Study of languages

The study of languages is called **linguistics**. Linguistics tells us there are two main parts of the languages we use every day:

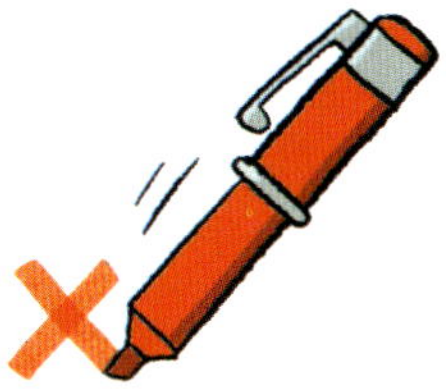

1. **Grammar** is the **set of rules** that set out the correct use of a language.

2. **Vocabulary** is the **set of known words** that make up a language.

History of languages

Different parts of the world use different spoken and written languages. There are different theories on how these languages came to be.

Some experts think that languages gradually evolved from the ways that our human ancestors communicated – for example, the gestures and sounds made by apes. Others think that languages are used *only* by humans and so appeared only after humans started to evolve.

However, it is generally accepted that languages were *spoken* before writing systems (such as alphabets) were created to *record* them.

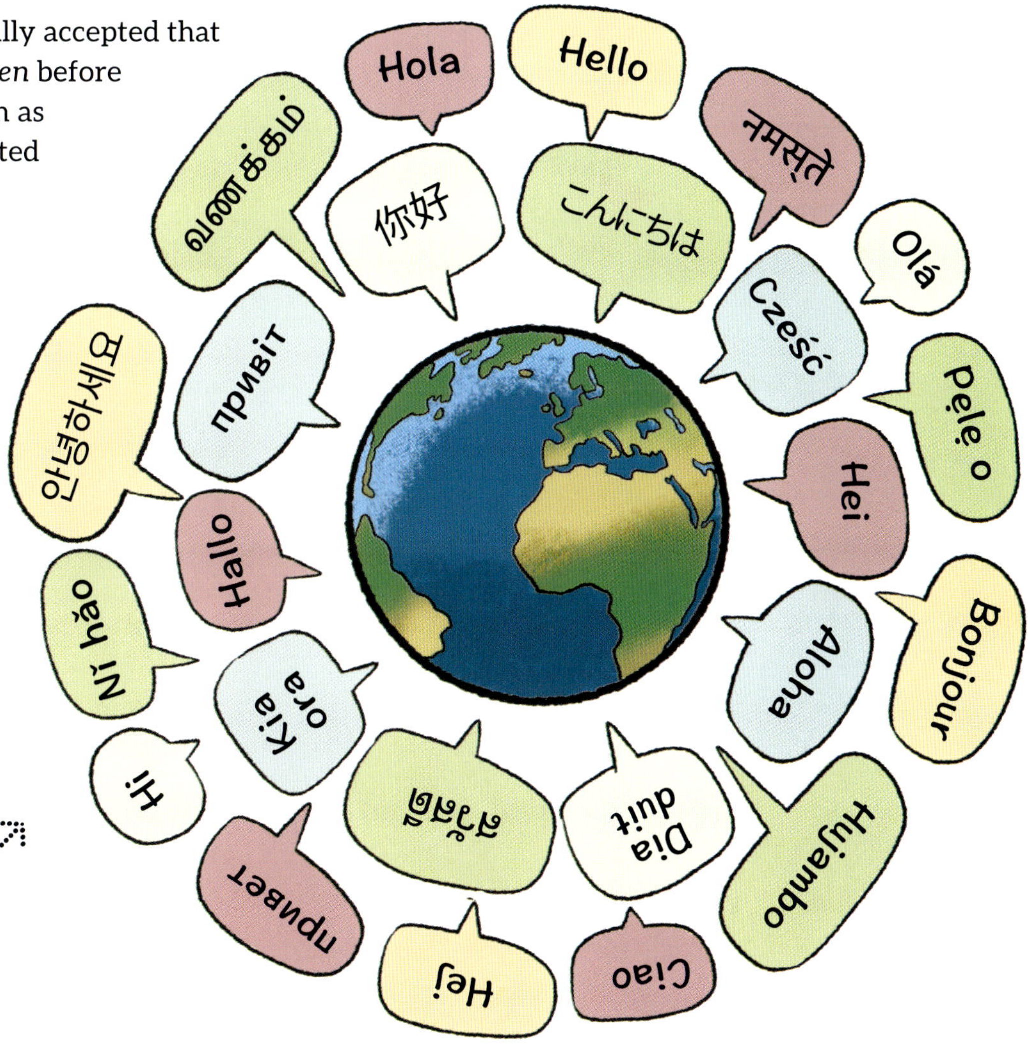

The word or words for 'hello' look and sound different in languages all around the world.

Languages can come naturally ...

We may not agree on how languages *first* came to be, but we do know that there are two ways languages are developed today. Let's start with natural languages.

When is a language *natural*?

A **natural** or **ordinary** language is one that has developed gradually through human use. Natural languages tend to change over time as humans learn and experience new things.

Examples of natural languages include English, Mandarin, Spanish, Kiswahili, Ukrainian and Tamil.

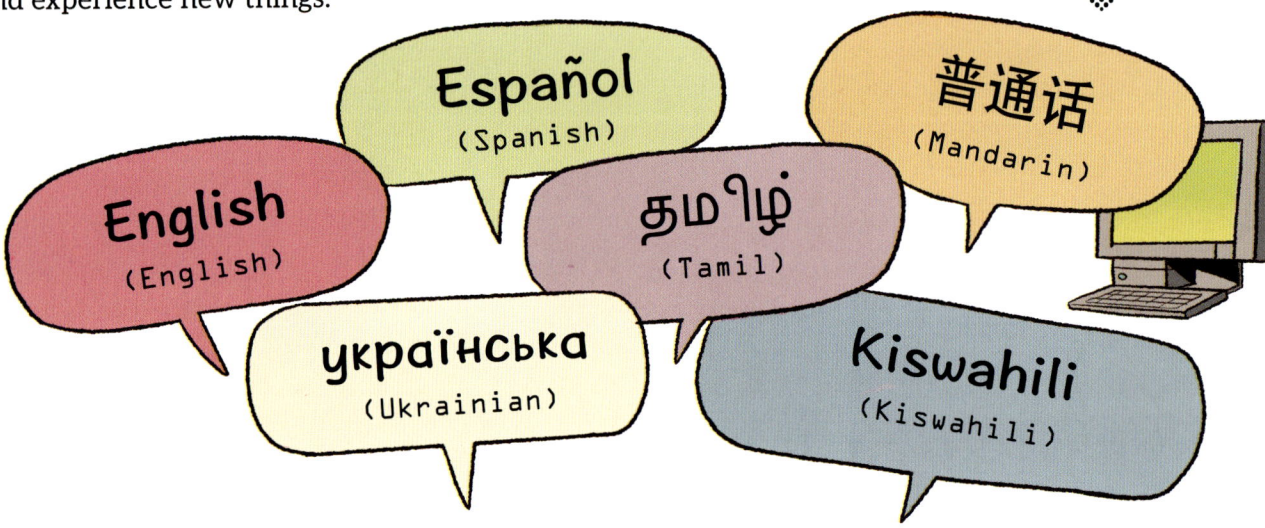

Forms of natural language

Natural language can be used in three ways:

1. When we talk to one another, we use the **spoken** form.
2. We can also **sign** a language using our hands to communicate.
3. When we want a more permanent record, we use the **written** form.

Waving a hand can be a sign for hello.

Written language

A **writing system** is a set of symbols that follow the rules of a language. Depending on the writing system, the symbols can stand for sounds, syllables or whole words. For example, in written English, each letter in the alphabet stands for a sound, but in written Japanese, each symbol represents a syllable in the word.

Written language can be set down in different media (formats), such as on paper or as electronic documents kept on computers.

Going digital

Natural languages are great for human communication. But a lot of information today is processed by computers, which don't have human brains. To communicate **precisely** with computers, we have developed constructed languages (see next page).

Human communication can confuse computers!

... or languages can be constructed

We need to be super-precise when communicating with computers. For this, we use constructed languages.

What makes a constructed language?

A constructed language is created for a specific use. Natural languages can be complex, so it can be easier to construct a language to express ideas more simply for our particular needs.

For example, **Láadan** is a language that is used exclusively to *research* languages!

Constructed languages can also be used as the language of a fantasy world in games, books, film and TV.

For example, the **Elvish** languages in the 1954 book, *The Lord of the Rings*, or the Na'vi language in the 2009 film, *Avatar*, are all constructed languages.

These Elvish words read, "I would like to speak with you, please".

Constructed languages can also be used to provide instructions to computers and other devices.

This is a simple program in a constructed language called Rust.

In this book, we will take a closer look at constructed languages for computer science (CS).

Languages for computer science

An important job of computer science is to make software (also called code or programs). Software are instructions for computers.

The people who make software are called software developers or software engineers. They do not simply write code from nothing. To make good software, they need to understand what the software need to do and the best way to do it.

This happens as a **life cycle** of stages, with a different output (product) at each stage.

SOFTWARE LIFE CYCLE: PLANNING, ANALYSIS, DESIGN, DEVELOPMENT, TESTING, RELEASE, MAINTENANCE

Constructed languages are used in many stages of this life cycle – both to write the software and to record the outputs.

Say hello!

Computer scientists have a tradition that the first program they write in any programming language begins with a test message: Hello, World!

Find out about an early programming language pioneer – John Backus – on page 28.

Language types for CS

When creating a language for CS, there is a lot to think about. What will it look like? What it will be used for? And who will use it?

Considering appearance

When you want to give someone directions, you can either draw them a map (**visual**) or write the route in words (**textual**). When we create software, we also write instructions in languages that are either textual or visual.

Here is a plan in **text** for a program to calculate someone's age.

```
Get date of birth
If the date is earlier than today
    Calculate age
    Display the age
If the date is not earlier than today
    Display a message saying that
    the date is not valid
```

We can also show the plan in a **visual flowchart**, which is a diagram that shows each step.

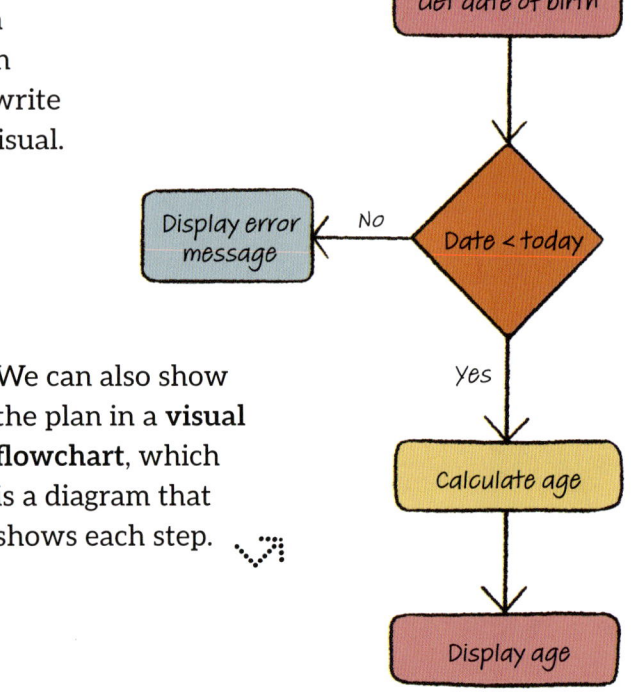

Considering the users

People are involved in many stages of the software life cycle (see page 9). Some, such as the software engineers themselves, are computer science experts. Others will only **use** or **sell** the software, and won't understand as much about it when they interact with it.

So, we have made constructed languages with different levels of detail to suit who is involved at each stage.

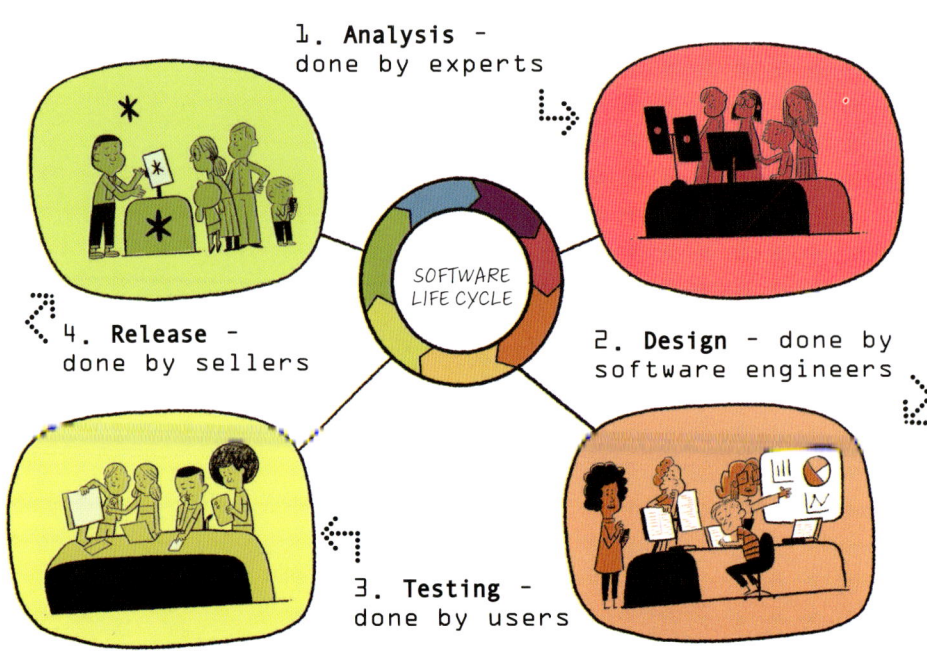

1. **Analysis** - done by experts
2. **Design** - done by software engineers
3. **Testing** - done by users
4. **Release** - done by sellers

SOFTWARE LIFE CYCLE

The ultimate language...

When software is finally run by computers, it is written in a language that is just a series of 0s and 1s. This language is called *binary code*. But binary code is very hard for humans – even computer scientists – to understand.

So, constructed languages that are easier for humans to understand are used in the development phase of the life cycle.

Natural language phrase

> I WOULD LIKE TO SPEAK WITH YOU, PLEASE ...
>
> 01001001 00100000 01110111 01101111
> 01110101 01101100 01100100 00100000
> 01101100 01101001 01101011 01100101
> 00100000 01110100 01101111 00100000
> 01110011 01110000 01100101 01100001
> 01101011 00100000 01110111 01101001
> 01110100 01101000 00100000 01111001
> 01101111 01110101 00100000 00100000
> 01110000 01101100 01100101 01100001
> 01110011 01100101 00100000 00101110
> 00101110 00101110

The same phrase converted to binary code

Language levels

When we look at the languages used in the process of making software, we can think of them on four levels:

- At the top, we can have some text in a **natural language** explaining what the software does.

  > LET'S BUILD A WEB APP FOR SCHOOL ANNOUNCEMENTS!
  >
  > Web client ↔ Web server ↔ App server ↔ Database

- Then computer scientists can use **modelling languages** to set out the important features of the software. This is part of the design stage, so modelling languages are often visual.

  > JavaScript

- Software engineers then write programs in **programming languages**, such as JavaScript. These are easier to work with than binary code.

  > 01100010 01101001
  > 01101110 01100001
  > 01110010 01111001

- This will then be translated into binary code by computer programs called **compilers** and **interpreters** (see page 23).

Even more languages!

Most computer software deals with data (singular: datum), which are details about things. Some constructed languages are very useful for managing data.

Markup languages

Data on a computer that haven't been organised or processed are called 'raw'. Raw data don't have a lot of meaning.

Markup languages are used to organise raw data. They also provide instructions for how the data should be used or displayed. These languages are used worldwide, so many different computer programs can use and update the data.

HTML (HyperText Markup Language) is a widely used markup language. It provides instructions for how the data for web pages should be shown in web browsers.

HTML text

```
<!DOCTYPE html>
<html>
<body>

<h1>Languages for Computer Science</h1>
<h2>Programming languages</h2>
<p>I love programming!</p>

</body>
</html>
```

This is how the HTML text appears to a user.

Languages for Computer Science

Programming languages

I love programming!

Data definition languages

Data definition languages (DDLs) can help organise data, wherever they are stored. Here we look at data that are kept in a collection called a **database**, which may store data as graphs or tables.

Table

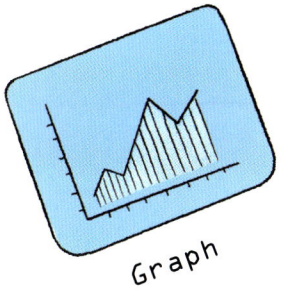
Graph

The data definition language SQL (Structured Query Language), for example, can be used to set up the structure of a table. Then data can be stored in the table.

AHHH, NICE AND TIDY AND READY FOR DATA.

```
CREATE TABLE person (
    first_name   VARCHAR (50),
    family_name  VARCHAR (50),
    date_of_birth DATE
)
```

Here is an example of using SQL to create a table to store the names and birth dates of people in a database.

And here is what it looks like as a table.

first_name	family_name	date_of_birth

Query languages

But to use all these data, we need a way to access to them! When a program looks for the data it needs in a database, we call it *querying* the database. Constructed languages called **query languages** are used for this.

IT'S LIKE MAGIC!

For example, if we fill our database table with some data, like this ...

first_name	family_name	date_of_birth
Mira	Smith	10-07-2012
Alejandro	Romero	22-01-2010
Yan	Li	05-11-2013

```
SELECT first_name, family_name
FROM person
WHERE date_of_birth > '31-12-2010'
```

... we can then use a query language (this is **SQL** again, which is also a query language!) to write a query. Let's ask the database who has a birthday after the end of 2010 ...

first_name	family_name
Mira	Smith
Yan	Li

... which will return these results.

It's all syntax and semantics

Constructed languages have to be set up (defined) very carefully, especially if the language has to be processed by a computer. This is because computers can't always guess what we want them to do if the meaning is unclear!

What is in a language definition?

In general, all natural and constructed language definitions have five parts:

1. **Morphology** – how words are formed
2. **Phonology** – how letters and sounds are related
3. **Syntax** – how words are combined to form phrases and sentences
4. **Semantics** – how meaning is expressed
5. **Pragmatics** – how the language is used.

For languages used in computer science, syntax and semantics are particularly important.

Morphology

Phonology

Syntax

Semantics

Pragmatics

Syntax

Syntax is part of a language's grammar – just like when you learn grammar in school. In computer science, syntax rules tell us how a language's letters and symbols can be put together to make usable content (called **valid** content). So, syntax is all about **structure** and not about meaning.

Here is a **valid** Python program that adds two numbers and prints out the sum:

```
number1 = 100
number2 = 250

sum = number1 + number2

print("Sum of", number1, " and ", number2 , " is ", sum)
```

If the program is changed as below, its **syntax** is **not valid** for Python:

```
number1 = 100
number2 = 250

sum = number1 plus number2

print(Sum of, number1, " and ", number2 , " is ", sum)
```

Note: the + symbol is now the word plus.

Note: the speech marks around the words Sum of have been removed.

Semantics

We also need to be sure that the **meaning** (or the result) of what we write is what we wanted. In programming languages, semantics tells us what a valid program will do when it is run on a computer.

This is what should result from the valid Python program, above:

Find out about a pioneer who developed programs that translated between programming languages – Grace Hopper – on page 28.

Sum of 100 and 250 is 350

Ways of programming

There are many ways to approach problem-solving, and we can write software in different ways that best solve each problem!

Approaching problems

When we have to solve a problem, we usually think about how to make it easier to solve.

For example, we can solve the problem by dividing it into smaller parts. First we solve the smaller parts and then put the solutions to those parts together.

Or we can solve a problem by using a method like SODAS. This is where we consider **these four** parts of a problem, in order, before trying out a solution.

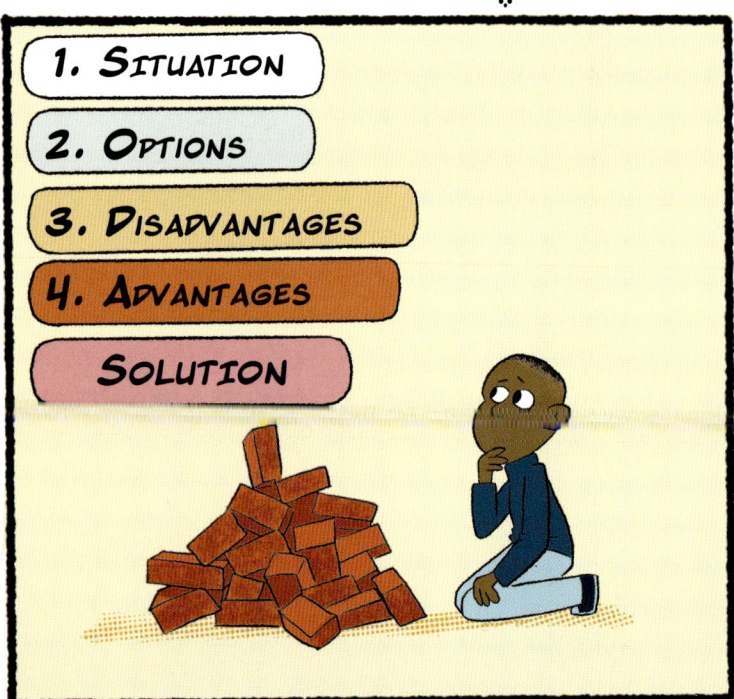

1. SITUATION
2. OPTIONS
3. DISADVANTAGES
4. ADVANTAGES

SOLUTION

Find out about a pioneer of problem-solving and programming languages for children – Seymour Papert – on page 29.

The perfect plan
Different types of problem need various ways of solving them. These ways are called **paradigms** (*pa-ruh-dimes*). Every new paradigm is based on:

- **Ideas** and **patterns** for thinking about the problem and solution
- How we **express** our thinking about it.

Programming paradigms

Programming paradigms can be grouped into two main types:

Imperative paradigms: programmers write down *all* the steps that the computer needs to take to solve the problem. So, programmers tell the computer what to do *and* how to do it.

Declarative paradigms: programmers write down *what* should happen but not *how* it is to happen. Helper programs (programs that support the programming process) will figure out how to do what the programmers want done.

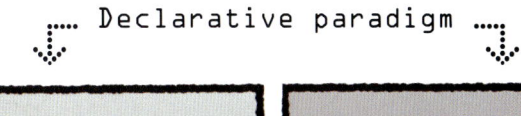

Languages for different paradigms

Many programming languages support one particular type of paradigm. Some of the common programming languages, such as Python, can be used to write programs in different paradigms.

Choose your language

Depending on the problem we want to solve, and the way (paradigm) in which we want to solve it, we will choose different programming languages.

Choosing a language

There are several things to think about when choosing your programming language. For example:

- Consider the **environment** in which the program will be run, such as on mobile devices, the web or desktop computers.

- Consider the **type of problem** to be solved, such as analysing data or developing a mobile application (app)

- Consider the **experience of the programmers**. If they have a lot of experience in a particular language, they can develop better code faster in that language.

- Consider the **qualities** expected from the program, such as how quickly it has to do its work.

Popular programming languages

These are some of the most popular programming languages and what they are often used for.

Smartphone app

For a smartphone app, **Kotlin** is often used because this language works on many different types of device.

Chatbots

Chatbots are for online help. **Python** is a popular choice because it offers a lot of support for software that uses artificial intelligence (AI).

Interactive website

For an interactive website, **HTML** and **JavaScript** are popular choices. This is because web pages can be written in HTML and JavaScript can work with HTML to respond to user actions, such as clicking a button or entering data in a form.

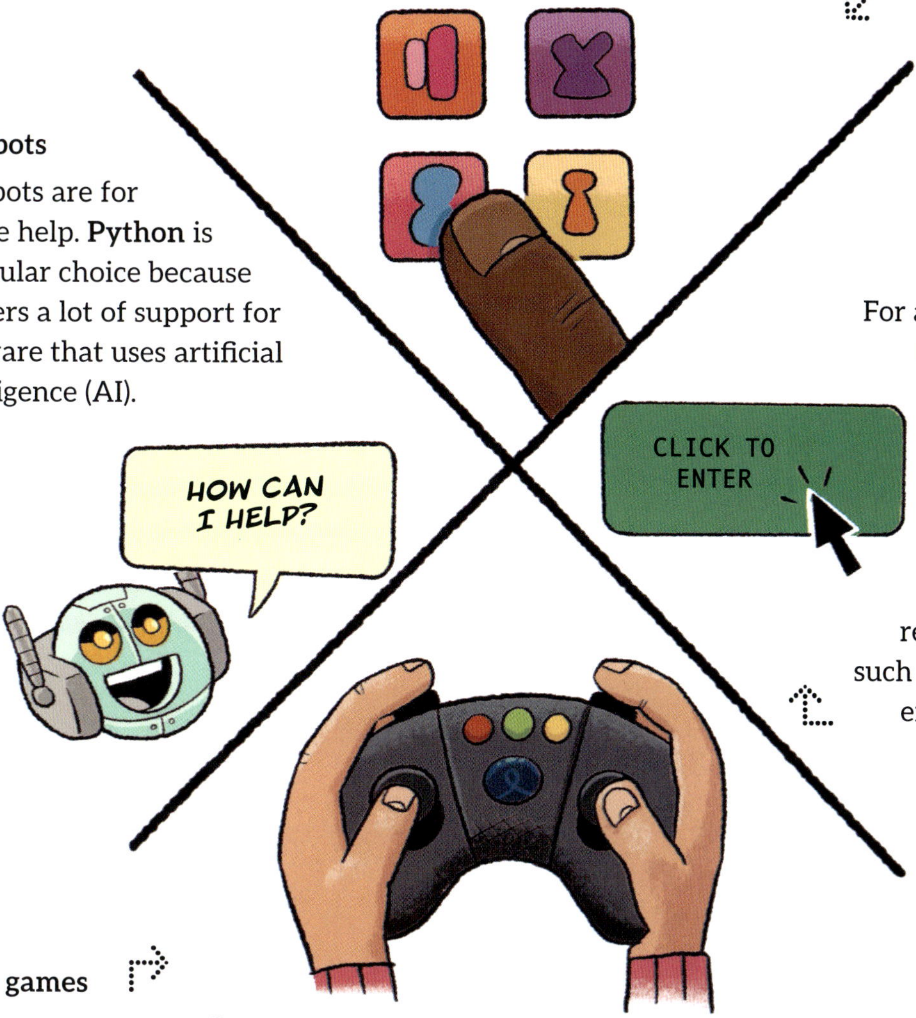

Video games

Video games may use **C++** because C++ programs can run fast. This is important in role-playing games so the game can react quickly to user actions. C++ also gives programmers more control over features.

Find out about the pioneer of the programming language C – Dennis Ritchie – on page 30.

Programming is a process

How can we go about writing programs and what happens after we write them?

Programming as a process

There are four main steps involved in solving a problem using software.

Step 1: planning

It is important to **plan** how we will build the software. Software engineers will often produce **design diagrams** when planning their work. This planning can be:

1. **Plan-driven:** making plans for the *complete* software from the start.

2. **Agile:** making just enough plans for *each section* of the software as it is built.

Step 2: programming

Based on these plans, software engineers will make programs that can be **run** (or **executed**) to solve the problem.

I LOVE TO RUN NEW SOFTWARE!

Step 3: testing

In order to check that a program solves a problem as expected, software engineers will run **tests**. This is a very important part of the development. Testing is done many times throughout the process of writing software to remove bugs (mistakes).

Step 4: user-testing

Once software engineers are satisfied that the program works correctly, they will test it with actual users to see whether it does what they want.

Bugs detected

De-bugged

Different languages for each step

Each step will use different languages.

Plans are usually done in **modelling languages** (see page 11).

Software and **tests** are written in **programming languages** (see page 11).

Software engineers will also write **guides** and **other documents** for users in **natural language** (see pages 6–7).

Find out about a pioneer of software engineering – Margaret Hamilton – on page 28.

Tools to make our work easier

More and more, computer scientists have to solve large, complex problems that need large, complex programs to be written. It is difficult for humans to create such programs correctly all by themselves, so they write more programs to help them!

Software tools

Computer scientists write these special programs, called **tools**, to help them write, run and correct other programs in a variety of ways.

Tools for WRITING code

Some tools that help to write code are basic editing programs. They help programmers format their code and save it as files so it's valid and usable.

Other tools are more advanced. They can automatically fill in some details in the code or highlight any mistakes made by human programmers.

Tools for RUNNING code

Tools called **compilers** translate programs into **intermediate** forms (in between the programming language and binary code).

Tools called **interpreters** translate code – in either programming languages or intermediate forms – into binary, and run the code.

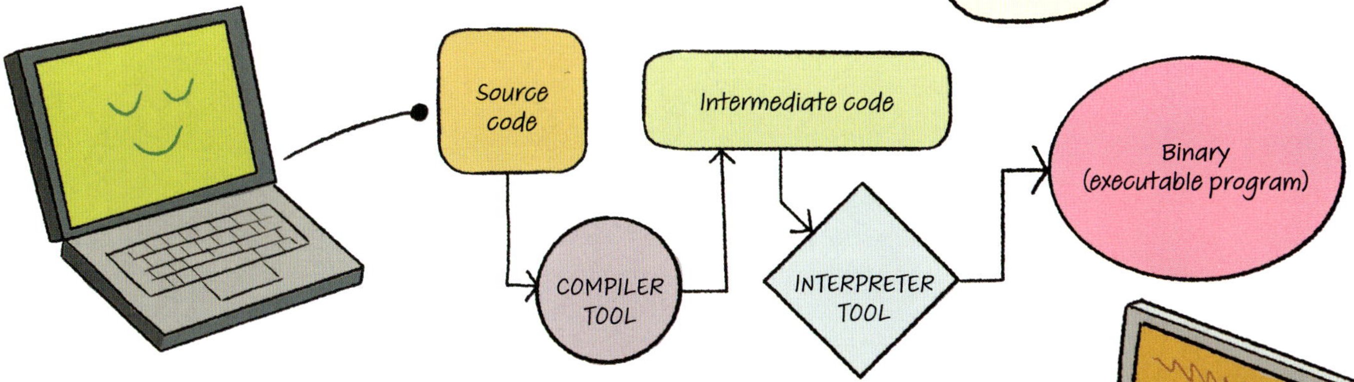

Tools for CHECKING code

When running code, software engineers might notice bugs. They can use tools called **debuggers** to try and find them.

Tools to put it all TOGETHER

Integrated Development Environments (IDEs) are tools that put all of these individual tools together into one big 'support environment' for software engineers. This means that engineers only have to use this one IDE tool and don't have to switch around among many tools.

IDE — Writing (basic and advanced) — Running — Debugging

Programs that write programs!

As well as all these tools, software engineers can also use tools that can write code themselves. (See more about this on pages 26–27.)

Case study: Blocks vs Python

We choose and use different languages for various reasons. Let's see how different a simple calculation can look in a visual language (Blocks) and a text language (Python)!

The problem to solve

Let's say we want to write a program that can find the **average of five numbers**.

We know how to do this ourselves using maths. We add the numbers together and divide the sum by the amount of numbers (five) to get the average.

If we want a **computer** to do the calculation, we will have to write down precise instructions for each step.

5 + 10 + 15 + 20 + 25 = 75

75 ÷ 5 = 15 [the average]

Block coding

Coding with blocks is a visual way of programming. Instead of writing all the code as text, we can drag and drop ready-made blocks to make the shape of the code we want and fill in the blanks with the data we need.

This is a bit like putting together a jigsaw puzzle. The blocks have to fit together properly to make valid code. This visual way of programming tends to be easier for beginners.

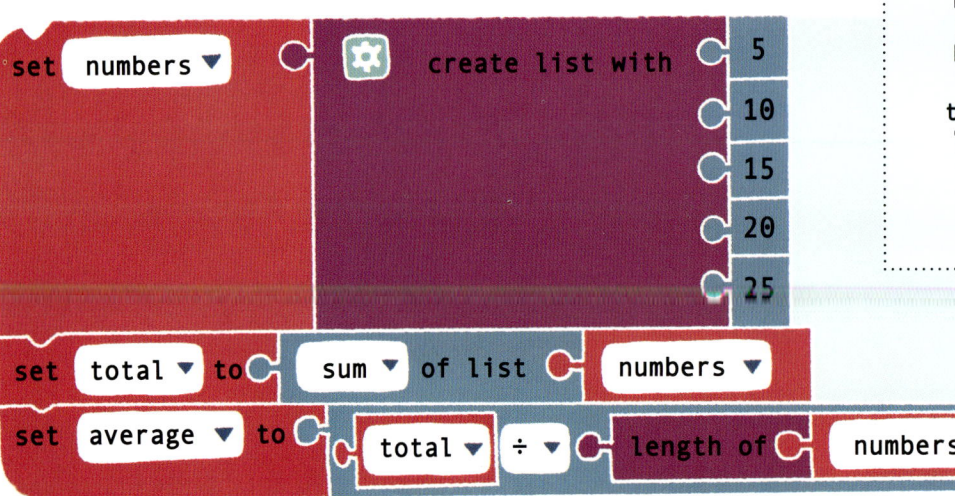

Python

Python provides some ready-made ways to help us do the maths in text form. These are called functions and do some useful work that we can use whenever we want.

First, we will put the numbers we want to average in a list called **numbers**.

NUMBERS

```
numbers = [5, 10, 15, 20, 25]
total = sum(numbers)
average = total / len(numbers)
```

SUM

To calculate the total of all the numbers in the list, we can use a ready-made function provided by Python. This function is called **sum**.

As the final step, we will divide the total by the length of the list to get the average of the numbers in the list.

Python also provides a ready-made function called **len** to find the length of a list.

LEN

Be creative!

So we see that maths and programming languages can be used to solve a problem in different ways. Both maths and programming are creative activities that are suitable for all kinds of people.

You choose

Can you see what is similar and what is different about the two programs?

Which of these programs do you like best? Why?

Let's imagine a new visual language for writing sandwich recipes. What pictures or symbols will it have? Can you write down a recipe for a jam sandwich in this language?

The future of programming languages

There are hundreds of programming languages – in different paradigms, for many purposes, and at various levels of detail. Where do we go from here?

Education makes a difference

In the early days of CS, there were not many people who could write programs. As CS has become more popular and is taught in schools and universities, there are lots more people who can write programs.

Future programmers

In the future, programming will be much more a part of everyday life. Many people will have some ability to create programs in their favourite languages with the help of tools. They may even come up with new languages to meet their needs.

Lean, green programming

As programming fills more of our lives, we will need languages and tools that will allow us to be 'greener' programmers.

Software engineers already build new systems by reusing or connecting existing programs. We can do this on a much larger scale to become more efficient with energy and development time.

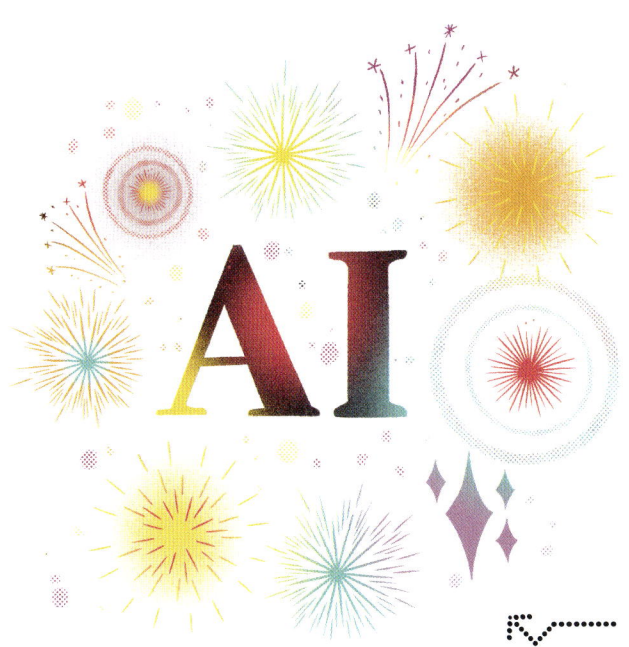

AI-generating programs

One of the biggest developments may be due to advances in AI.

At the moment, AI-generated code is not always reliable, because AI tools don't understand the problems they are trying to solve. They simply reuse, adapt or combine parts of programs they have seen before.

However, with further advances, it is possible that we may have reliable programs generated by AI. This would mean human programmers are free to focus on more creative and complex problems.

The software we want

Developments in CS and AI can lead to a future in which we can give a verbal command to a smart assistant, which can then create the programs we want, whenever we want them. For example, if we think of a new game we want to play, we can get a smart assistant to program it for us straight away.

HOW CAN I HELP?

PLEASE WRITE A PROGRAM FOR A NEW SPACE ADVENTURE GAME.

Quantum computing

We are also likely to see new programming languages for use in quantum computing. This type of computing uses physics to solve super-complex problems very fast.

Pioneer portraits

John Backus (1924-2007)

... was an American computer scientist, who designed and implemented the programming language FORTRAN (FORmula TRANslation). FORTRAN was one of the early and most widely used programming languages aimed at scientists. Backus, along with Peter Naur, also defined the Backus-Naur Form (BNF), which is a set of symbols used for defining the grammar of programming languages.

Margaret Hamilton (1936-)

... was the lead software engineer on NASA's Apollo Program which led to the first landing on the Moon. She came up with the name 'software engineering' to highlight that writing software should be an engineering discipline too. She proposed one of the first modelling languages as a way to reduce errors in software development.

Grace Hopper (1906-1992)

... developed the first compiler (a program to translate between programming languages) and contributed to the development of modern-day programming languages. She was a Rear Admiral in the US Navy and a teacher and communicator who helped people understand the benefits of modern technology.

Ross Ihaka (1954-)

... is a statistician (someone who collects and studies numbers about people, events or situations) from New Zealand who has Māori–European heritage. He and Robert Gentleman created the R programming language. R is widely used by scientists in many fields to analyse and visualise data.

Joseph Marie Jacquard (1752-1834)

... was a French merchant who developed the first programmable loom, which is a machine for weaving cloth.

Donald Knuth (1938-)

... is an American computer scientist and mathematician, who is well known for his work on algorithms and programming languages. He wrote a very famous series of books called *The Art of Computer Programming*.

Barbara Liskov (1939-)

... is an American computer scientist who has made many contributions to programming languages, operating systems and distributed computing, which is the method of making multiple computers work together to solve a common problem. Her work is used in many modern-day programming languages.

Yukihiro Matsumoto (1965-)

... is a Japanese computer scientist who created the Ruby programming language. Ruby can be used to write programs in different paradigms. Matsumoto is also known for his support for making software freely available (open source).

Seymour Papert (1928-2016)

... was a South-African born computer scientist and educator, who came up with the Logo programming language to help children learn coding. He created a small Logo robot in the form of a turtle, which could be used to draw designs on paper. His work on learning and teaching programming is still used today.

Continued on next page ...

29

Dennis Ritchie (1941-2011)

... was an American computer scientist, who was the main designer of the programming language C, still widely used today. He also worked on the Unix operating system and the B programming language, which was developed before C.

Maurice Wilkes (1913-2010)

... was an English computer scientist, who developed one of the first stored-program computers, which stored their programs in accessible memory. His ideas also contributed to modern high-level programming languages.

Further information

Books to read:

Why AI? by Dr Dharini Balasubramaniam (Wayland, 2024)
For a deeper dive into the details and debates around artificial intelligence

Super Tech (series) by Clive Gifford (Wayland, 2024)
For information about technology in space, gross tech, robots, AI and even dinosaurs!

Places to visit:

The National Museum of Computing
www.tnmoc.org/

Science Museum
www.sciencemuseum.org.uk

Centre for Computing History
www.computinghistory.org.uk

Science and Industry Museum
www.scienceandindustrymuseum.org.uk

Websites to visit:

www.kodable.com introduces young children to coding.

https://lightbot.com is an app that teaches programming concepts through puzzles.

https://developers.google.com/blockly#learn-with-blockly This Blockly site has links to Scratch, Blockly games and other hands-on programming sites.

https://snap.berkeley.edu is another block-coding site for kids.

Glossary

algorithm a set of instructions or steps to be followed in solving a problem or completing a task

ancestor a family member who lived long ago

application (app) a computer program produced for a specific purpose

artificial intelligence (AI) computer programs that imitate how humans make decisions and solve problems

binary code a program that is made up of 0s and 1s

code a computer program

compiler a software tool that checks the correctness of programs and translates them into intermediate forms (between programs and binary code)

computer science the study of, or information related to, computations and how far computations can be automated

computer scientist someone who has studied computer science and works in this area

constructed language a language created for a specific reason

data details we collect and store about things that help with completing tasks or solving problems

data definition language (DDL) a language that can help organise data wherever they are stored

evolve to change or develop slowly over time

format to arrange according to a given pattern

instruction a command given to a computer, as part of a computer program

intelligence the ability to gain knowledge and skills, and to use them in a logical and sensible way

intermediate between two other things

interpreter a software tool that translates code – in a programming language or intermediate form – into binary and runs it

language a system for exchanging ideas and information, and expressing thoughts and views

life cycle an ordered collection of all the stages something goes through during its existence or lifetime

linguistics the study of languages

markup language a language used to organise data with instructions for using or displaying the data

model a way of representing a real-life thing or situation, but usually without all the details

modelling language a language used to show the important features of a software, usually in a visual form

natural language a language that has evolved naturally through human use

online being available via a computer network, which is a collection of connected computers or devices that can exchange data with one another

output data produced by a computer program

paradigm a way of thinking about and solving a problem

pioneer one of the first people to do something

process a series of steps taken to achieve a goal

program a set of instructions written for a computer to carry out

programming language a language defined by computer scientists for writing computer programs

quantum computing a branch of computer science that uses ideas from physics to solve very complex problems very fast

query a request for data that meet the specified conditions

raw data unorganised or unprocessed data

record a way data are noted down for long-term use. In computer science, a record usually means a collection of related data, each potentially of a different type, used to describe or identify something specific

robot a machine that can complete tasks with little or no human involvement

scholar someone who studies a subject or topic

semantics meanings that can be expressed in languages

smart assistant an AI program that can complete different tasks based on voice commands from users

software a set of programs used for a specific purpose, such as operating a computer or completing a task

software engineering an organised way to create software, following good principles and practices

syntax a set of rules that decides how words can be combined correctly in a language

technology the result of applying science to practical problems to produce solutions

valid something that satisfies rules or can be accepted

writing system a set of symbols that follow the rules of a language

Quiz yourself!

1. Which of these is a constructed language?
   a) English
   b) Python
   c) Mandarin
   d) Spanish

2. Which of these steps is important for making software?
   a) Planning
   b) Coding
   c) Testing
   d) All of the above

3. Why do we need languages at different levels for computer science?
   a) Languages are used for different purposes in computer science, both by people and computers
   b) It is more interesting to have lots of languages
   c) Different people like to use different languages
   d) We don't need languages at different levels

4. Which of these is not important when choosing a programming language?
   a) The problem we want to solve
   b) How experienced the programmer is in a language
   c) The name of the language
   d) The kinds of device the program will run on

5. Which types of language do we use to get data from a database?
   a) Modelling languages
   b) Natural languages
   c) Markup languages
   d) Query languages

Answers are at the bottom of the page.

Index

algorithms 29
apps 11, 18, 19
artificial intelligence (AI) 19, 27

Backus, John 9, 28
binary code 11, 23
bugs (mistakes) 21, 23

communication 4, 5, 7, 8, 28
compilers 11, 23, 28
computers 7, 8, 11, 12, 14, 15, 17, 18, 24, 29, 30
computer science (CS) 8-11, 15, 26-30
constructed languages 7-14

data 12, 13, 18, 19, 24, 28
database 13
data definition languages 13

Gentleman, Robert 28
grammar 5, 15, 28

Hamilton, Margaret 21, 28
Hopper, Grace 15, 28

Ihaka, Ross 28
interpreters 11, 23

Jacquard, Joseph Marie 29

Knuth, Donald 29

Liskov, Barbara 29

markup languages 12
Matsumoto, Yukihiro 29
modelling languages 11, 21, 28

natural languages 6-8, 11, 14, 21
Naur, Peter 28

Papert, Seymour 16, 29
paradigms 17, 18, 26, 29
problem-solving 16-18, 20-22, 25, 27, 29
programming languages 9-11, 15-19, 21, 23-30
  C++ 19
  FORTRAN 28
  HTML 12, 19
  JavaScript 11, 19

Kotlin 19
Logo 29
Python 15, 17, 19, 24, 25
R 28
Ruby 29

quantum computing 27
query languages 13

Ritchie, Dennis 19, 30
rules (of a language) 7, 15

software 9-12, 19-23, 26-28, 29
symbols 7, 15, 25, 28

tools 22, 23, 26, 27

valid content 15, 22, 24
visual way of programming 24, 25

Quiz answers: 1. b; 2. d; 3. a; 4. c; 5. d